SUPER SCIENCE INFOGRAPHICS

FORCES AND MOTION THROUGH INFOGRAPHICS

Rebecca Rowell

graphics by
Venitia Dean

Lerner Publications Company
Minneapolis

Lerner Publications Company
A division of Lerner Publishing Group, Inc.
241 First Avenue North
Minneapolis, MN U.S.A. 55401

Website address: www.lernerbooks.com

Main text set in Univers LT Std 12/15.
Typeface provided by Adobe Systems.

Library of Congress Cataloging-in-Publication Data
Rowell, Rebecca.
  Forces and motion through infographics / by Rebecca Rowell.
    pages   cm — (Super science infographics)
  Includes index.
  ISBN 978-1-4677-1291-0 (lib. bdg. : alk. paper)
  ISBN 978-1-4677-1786-1 (eBook)
  1. Force and energy—Juvenile literature. 2. Motion"Juvenile literature. I. Title.
  QC73.4.R683 2014
  530—dc23   2013004392

Manufactured in the United States of America
1 – BP – 7/15/13

CONTENTS

RULERS OF THE UNIVERSE

Do you have a future in physics?
To find out, take this test.

1. Do you wonder how basically everything moves?

2. Do you like working with math and numbers?

3. Is riding a roller coaster a science experiment to you?

4. How about gravity? Are you drawn to it?

Did you answer yes to any of those questions?

CONGRATULATIONS!

You have what it takes to be a budding physicist—a scientist who studies forces and motion. There's so much to study too. Earth and everything in the universe is moving. And forces make that motion happen. They're the two rulers of the universe. Studying everything in the universe isn't easy. There's always more and more data about the way things move and the forces at work. And new data means more questions. It can make your head spin!

Physicists use graphs, charts, and other infographics to help sort through all the information. These graphics can make those big, mysterious ideas a bit clearer. Are you ready to join in the fun? Let's get moving!

CONSTANT MOTION

You are always on the move—even if you are standing still. Earth is doing all the moving. It's in constant motion. It's hard to believe, isn't it? Let's take a closer look at motion!

WHAT IS MOTION?

Motion is when something moves. Here are the two kinds of motion:

1. **TRANSLATION** is when an object moves on a line or a curve. Earth orbits the sun. It moves along a curved line around the sun.

2. **ROTATION** is the other type of motion. It's when an object spins around its center of gravity. Earth does that too. It spins around its center axis.

It takes energy to make motion happen. Potential energy is stored energy. When it is used to make motion, it becomes kinetic energy. That is energy that is being used.

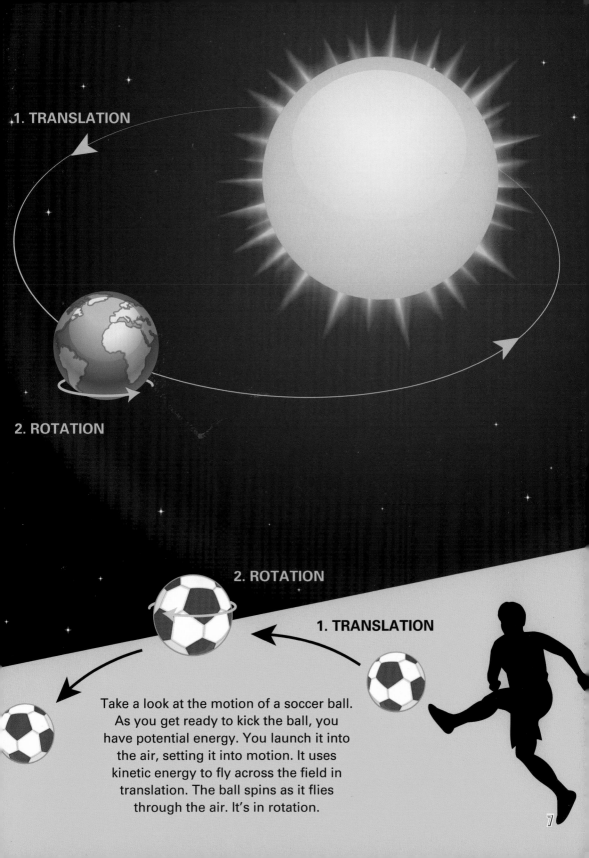

1. TRANSLATION

2. ROTATION

2. ROTATION

1. TRANSLATION

Take a look at the motion of a soccer ball. As you get ready to kick the ball, you have potential energy. You launch it into the air, setting it into motion. It uses kinetic energy to fly across the field in translation. The ball spins as it flies through the air. It's in rotation.

WHEEL OF FORCES

You can't always see them, but you can see what they do. Sound mysterious, don't they? They're forces: different types of pushes or pulls. Different forces affect motion in different ways. Sometimes the force is you. Sometimes the force is acting upon you. And many times, more than one force is applied at the same time. Spin the wheel to check out some of the different forces at work in the universe.

balanced forces

unbalanced forces

BALANCED AND UNBALANCED FORCES

Forces are balanced or unbalanced. When they're balanced, they're equal. When they're unbalanced, they're unequal.

A sled can show both balanced and unbalanced forces. At the top of a hill, gravity pulls down on the sled and the ground pushes up in equal forces. When the sled moves, friction pulls the sled down the hill.

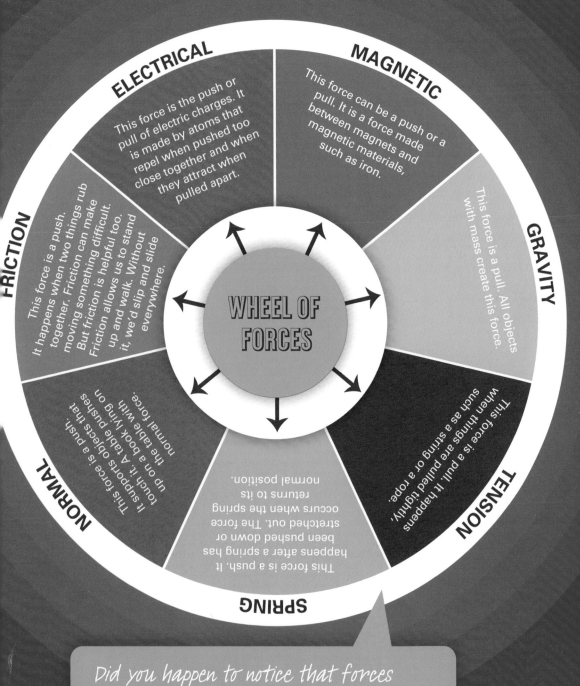

WHEEL OF FORCES

ELECTRICAL
This force is the push or pull of electric charges. It is made by atoms that repel when pushed too close together and they attract when pulled apart.

MAGNETIC
This force can be a push or a pull. It is a force made between magnets and magnetic materials, such as iron.

GRAVITY
This force is a pull. All objects with mass create this force.

FRICTION
This force is a push. It happens when two things rub together. Friction can make moving something difficult. But friction is helpful too. Friction allows us to stand up and walk. Without it, we'd slip and slide everywhere.

TENSION
This force is a pull. It happens when things are pulled tightly, such as a string or a rope.

NORMAL
This force is a push. It supports objects that touch it. A table pushes up on the table lying on the table (normal force).

SPRING
This force is a push. It happens after a spring has been pushed down or stretched out. The force occurs when the spring returns to its normal position.

Did you happen to notice that forces require two objects to interact? They do!

⑨

KINGS OF GRAVITY

We all feel the effects of gravity. But gravity wasn't understood until Isaac Newton and Albert Einstein came along. Newton first thought about how gravity acted. And Einstein built upon that knowledge, figuring out what caused gravity. Take a look at how these two brilliant scientists changed the way we think about gravity.

ISAAC NEWTON

Isaac Newton (1642–1727) was an English physicist and mathematician. He realized that the gravity holding objects to Earth's surface extended far above Earth. He believed that the same gravity held the moon in Earth's orbit. He called this his law of universal gravitation. This theory looked at how gravity worked through space, or distance.

Newton's idea described the strength of gravity very well. He knew it existed and was strong enough to hold planets in orbit around the sun. His theory had a problem, though. He couldn't explain how gravity worked.

Newton showed that gravity is the force that kept the moon in Earth's orbit.

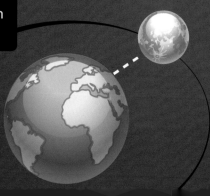

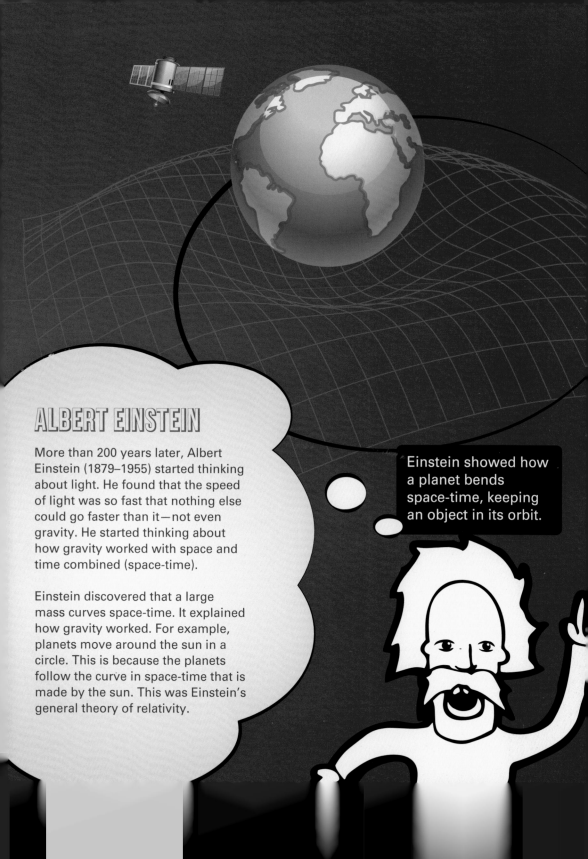

ALBERT EINSTEIN

More than 200 years later, Albert Einstein (1879–1955) started thinking about light. He found that the speed of light was so fast that nothing else could go faster than it—not even gravity. He started thinking about how gravity worked with space and time combined (space-time).

Einstein discovered that a large mass curves space-time. It explained how gravity worked. For example, planets move around the sun in a circle. This is because the planets follow the curve in space-time that is made by the sun. This was Einstein's general theory of relativity.

Einstein showed how a planet bends space-time, keeping an object in its orbit.

OLLIE ANATOMY

Skateboarding tricks are all about physics. Forces rule how fast a skater can go. They also rule how much air a skater can get. The Ollie is a basic skateboarding trick. It's one that every good skater needs to master before trying harder tricks. Check out the physics involved with the Ollie.

arrows = force

Before the trick starts, forces are already in action. The weight of the skater pushes down on the board. Earth's gravity pulls down on the board. And the ground also pushes up on the board. The skater crouches down on the board. A low center of mass will help him get more air on the jump.

The skater pushes the board forward. It moves faster and faster. Now it's time for the trick. The skater straightens his legs and raises his arms. This makes the skater's rear foot push down on the tail of the board. The rear foot has more force pushing down than the front foot. The nose of the board lifts up.

The tail hits the ground. The ground pushes with upward force on the tail. This makes the board bounce up.

In the air, the skater drags his front foot forward. It scratches against the rough surface. This causes friction.

LAWS OF MOTION

Remember Isaac Newton? He thought about motion too, not just gravity.

He developed three laws of motion. The laws are about how objects interact. The objects can be great or small, from massive planets to tiny atoms. They apply to people too, including you. These are his three laws of motion:

1. An object at rest or in motion stays that way until acted on by a force. An object will not accelerate until a force acts upon it. An object stays at rest or moving at the same speed in the same direction—until acted upon by a force.
2. Force = mass × acceleration. The more force put on an object, the greater the acceleration. Also, the same force put on objects of different mass causes different amounts of acceleration.
3. For every action, there's an equal and opposite reaction.

The skater starts pushing his front foot down on the nose. He pulls his rear foot up at the same time. The rear wheels go up, and the board straightens out.

The board and skater use gravity to fall back down to the ground.

The board hits the ground. The force of the ground pushes back on the board. The skater bends his legs. It helps the force spread out in his body. His legs might be hurt if he does not do this.

FAST, FASTER, FASTEST

It's fun to go really fast! Ever try it on your bike? Speed is how fast something is moving. To find speed, you need to know how long it took something to get from one point to another. And you need to know the distance that was traveled. There's an equation for determining speed. It is speed = distance/time.

Check out these amazingly fast speedsters.

mph = miles per hour
kph = kilometers per hour

Fastest Human—Usain Bolt: 28 mph (45 kph)

Fastest Land Animal—Cheetah: 64 mph (103 kph)

Fastest Car: 267 mph (430 kph)

Fastest Train: 302 mph (486 kph)

Sound: 741 mph (1,193 kph)

Earth's orbit: 67,062 mph (107,925 kph)

Light: 670,615,200 mph (1,079,250,548 kph)

ROLLER COASTER THRILLS

Twists, turns, upside-down rolls, and terrifying plunges. They're all part of a thrilling roller coaster ride. But how come riders don't fall out of the cars? And why do the cars stay on the tracks? It's because forces, energy, and inertia are at work.

Roller coasters don't have engines. A cable or a lift pulls the cars to the top of the first hill. The cars gather lots of potential energy on the way up. The higher the hill is, the more energy that is stored. And if the cars have more energy, they will move really fast on the track.

Now it's time for kinetic energy to take over. Gravity pulls the cars. They speed down the hill. Friction from the cars' wheels helps keep the cars on the track. The cars gather enough energy to make it to the top of the next hill. And Newton's first law kicks in too. Inertia keeps the cars moving up the hill.

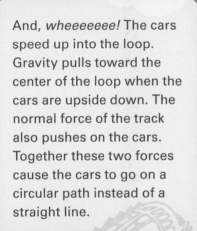

And, *wheeeeeee!* The cars speed up into the loop. Gravity pulls toward the center of the loop when the cars are upside down. The normal force of the track also pushes on the cars. Together these two forces cause the cars to go on a circular path instead of a straight line.

The cars lose energy toward the end of the track. Wind and friction on the track slows down the ride. The cars can only get up smaller hills now. Then brakes at the end of the ride stop the cars. Time to get out!

POWERFUL MAGNETS

You can find magnets in just about every machine. They're hidden inside most of the things we use every day. But not all magnets are the same. Some are extremely powerful, and some are very weak. Take a look at some of the strengths of different magnets.

AMAZING MAGLEV TRAINS

Some trains don't even have engines. Instead, strong magnets and an electric current power them. The trains glide on air. It makes for a smooth and incredibly fast ride. Most can reach speeds from 150 to 250 mph (240 to 400 kph). They're quieter than regular trains and better for the environment too. Here's how magnets and electric current make these trains work:

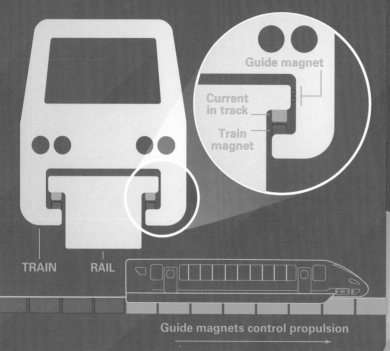

Guide magnet

Current in track

Train magnet

TRAIN

RAIL

Guide magnets control propulsion

The 45 Tesla Hybrid (strongest research magnet at the National High Magnetic Field Laboratory)

45 T

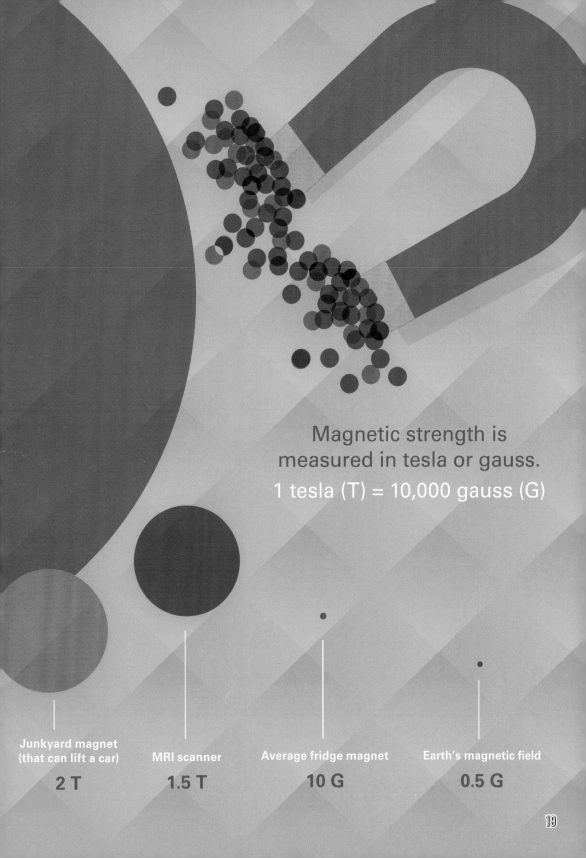

Magnetic strength is measured in tesla or gauss.

1 tesla (T) = 10,000 gauss (G)

Junkyard magnet (that can lift a car)

2 T

MRI scanner

1.5 T

Average fridge magnet

10 G

Earth's magnetic field

0.5 G

SURVIVING A NASCAR CRASH

If you drive fast, you can crash hard. And Nascar cars reach some of the highest speeds possible. Car crashes are part of the sport. Crashes are also examples of Newton's laws of motion in action. Here's how specially designed Nascar cars and other safety devices keep drivers safe during crashes.

1 Kinetic energy and speed have a lot to do with each other. The faster a car goes, the more kinetic energy it has.

2 A crash stops the forward motion of the car. But there is a lot of kinetic energy in the car. It has to be released. It becomes heat and sound, and is transferred to different parts of the car.

3 The energy has to go somewhere. A Nascar car is designed to control where that energy goes. It has crumple zones at the front and rear of the car.

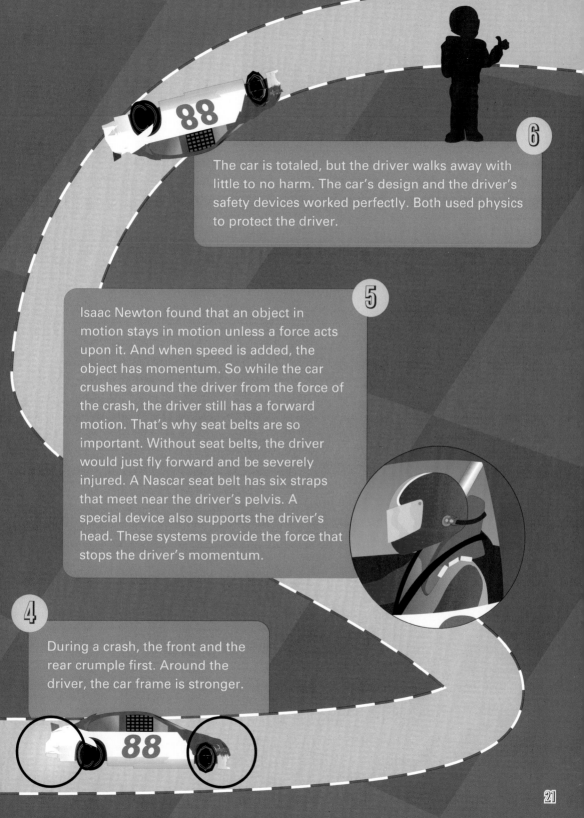

6

The car is totaled, but the driver walks away with little to no harm. The car's design and the driver's safety devices worked perfectly. Both used physics to protect the driver.

5

Isaac Newton found that an object in motion stays in motion unless a force acts upon it. And when speed is added, the object has momentum. So while the car crushes around the driver from the force of the crash, the driver still has a forward motion. That's why seat belts are so important. Without seat belts, the driver would just fly forward and be severely injured. A Nascar seat belt has six straps that meet near the driver's pelvis. A special device also supports the driver's head. These systems provide the force that stops the driver's momentum.

4

During a crash, the front and the rear crumple first. Around the driver, the car frame is stronger.

10 JOBS FOR SIMPLE MACHINES

Do you ever think, *that's too hard; I wish I could make it easier?* A simple machine may be just the thing you need. Simple machines are the basic tools that make work easier. They are in lots of tools that you use every day. Check out some of the cool jobs that are made easier with simple machines.

THE SIX SIMPLE MACHINES

These six simple machines are used in millions of ways.

 Inclined Plane

 Wedge

 Screw

 Lever

 Pulley

 Wheel and Axle

Chop some firewood for a chilly winter day. A wedge on the ax splits the wood.

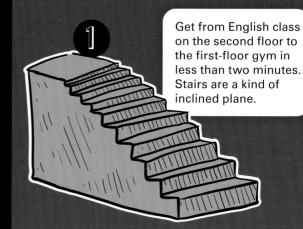

Get from English class on the second floor to the first-floor gym in less than two minutes. Stairs are a kind of inclined plane.

4

Get a cool drink of water next time you're in the country. A pulley in a well makes it easy to bring up a bucket.

5

Keep the strawberry jelly in and the ants out! Jar lids use a screw system to stay on.

3

Raise the flag high on the Fourth of July. A pulley makes this work easy.

6

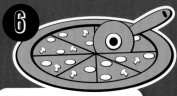

Cut yourself a big slice of pepperoni pizza. A rolling pizza cutter is a sharp wheel and axle.

No more excuses! Keep your homework from flying away in the wind. Staple it together. A stapler is a kind of lever.

7

Shed some light on the night. Put a new lightbulb in a lamp. A screw keeps it in place.

8

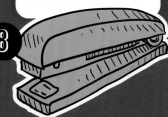

9

Cruise through the city on your lowrider bike. It uses a wheel and axle to work.

10

Move your enormous fossil collection. An inclined plane is a great way to move heavy things. They can go from low to high points with ease.

TWINKLE, TWINKLE, LITTLE SATELLITE

Just turn on the television or make a call on a cell phone. You are instantly accessing information sent by a satellite. The sky is full of these complex machines. Satellites use two or more simple machines. That's what makes them complex. More than 1,000 satellites orbit Earth. The United States has the most satellites—more than 400 of them. Here's a close-up view of these complex machines.

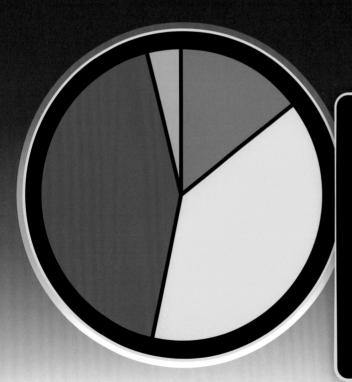

A SKY FULL OF SATELLITES

The United States owns many of the satellites in space. Here's what they are used for.

- Commercial: 200 (44%)
- Government: 116 (26%)
- Military: 128 (28%)
- Civil: 11 (2%)

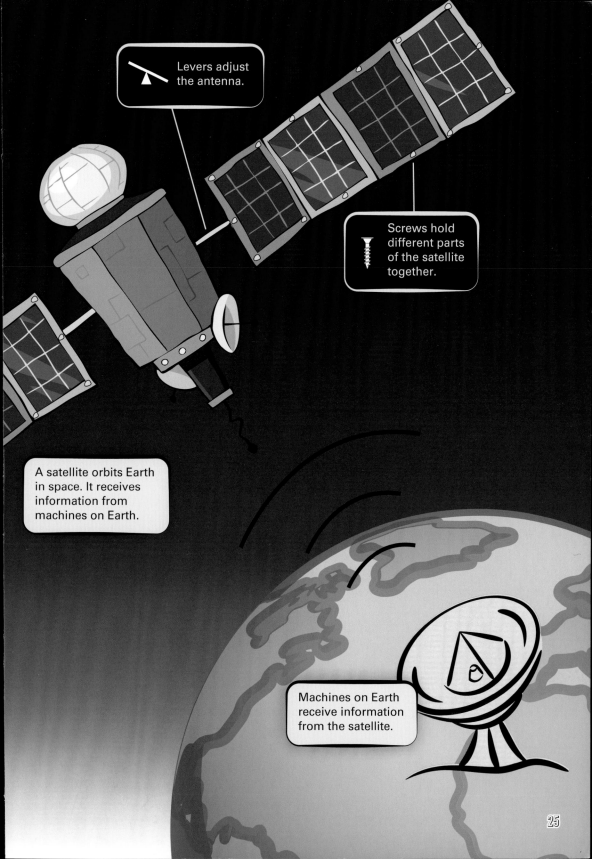

ROCKET POWER

Breaking away from Earth's gravity isn't easy. Rocket scientists know all about that. That is one of their biggest challenges when designing rockets meant to go to space. Guess where they began? With Isaac Newton and his equations about gravity, force, mass, and acceleration. Here's how rocket design makes use of Newton's ideas.

Gravity's force near Earth's surface pulls down on the rocket. The rocket must move at a faster rate than gravity. If it doesn't, it will not make it high enough to escape gravity's pull. The higher the rocket gets, the weaker gravity's pull is.

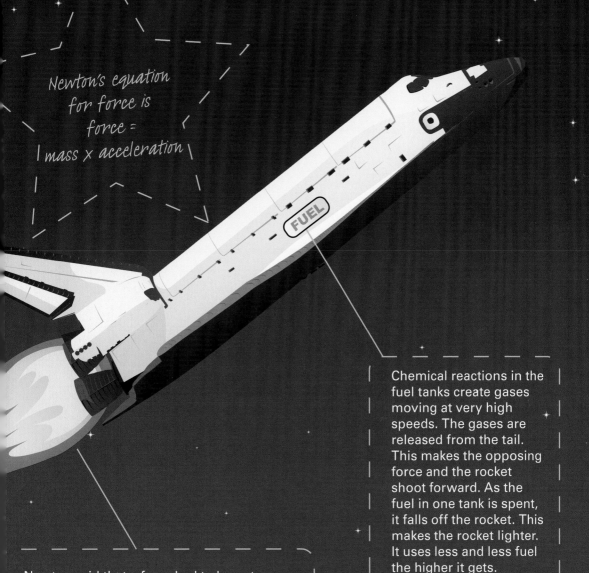

Newton's equation
for force is
force =
mass × acceleration

FUEL

Chemical reactions in the fuel tanks create gases moving at very high speeds. The gases are released from the tail. This makes the opposing force and the rocket shoot forward. As the fuel in one tank is spent, it falls off the rocket. This makes the rocket lighter. It uses less and less fuel the higher it gets.

Newton said that a force had to be put upon a mass to make it accelerate. Newton also said that every force has an equal and opposite force. For rockets, this means that the force of the gas shot down from a rocket equals the force pushing it forward. Scientists measure the amount of gas and at what speed it is pushed out. From this and the mass of the rocket, they can figure out what speed the rocket will move forward.

BUOYANT SUBMARINES

It doesn't make a whole lot of sense. Very heavy ships and submarines should sink in the ocean, shouldn't they? But they don't. That's because of buoyancy and density.

When an object is in water, some water is displaced. The weight of that water is the buoyant force on the object. The density of an object is its mass divided by its volume.

For an object less dense than water, the buoyant force can be larger than the object's weight. This lifts it partly out of the water. But an object more dense than water will sink. Its buoyant force is less than the object's weight. If the object has the same density as water, its weight equals the buoyant force. It neither rises nor sinks.

Submarines need to be able to control their buoyancy. Here's how they do it:

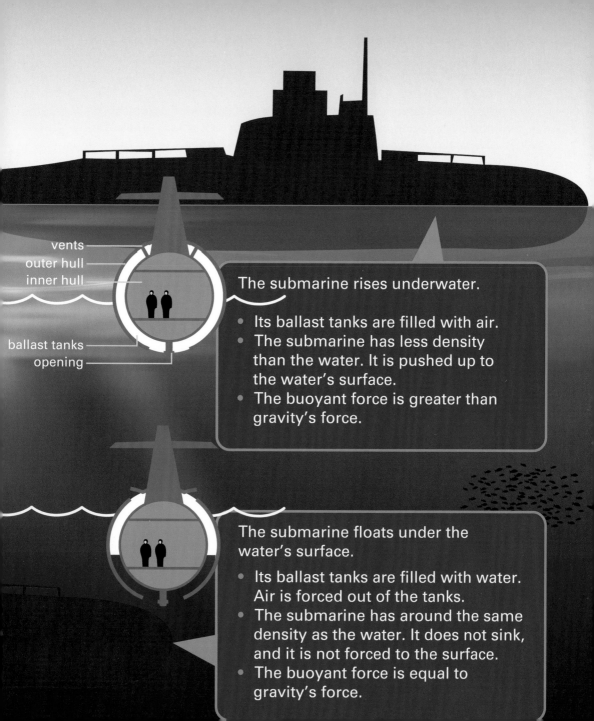

vents
outer hull
inner hull

ballast tanks
opening

The submarine rises underwater.

- Its ballast tanks are filled with air.
- The submarine has less density than the water. It is pushed up to the water's surface.
- The buoyant force is greater than gravity's force.

The submarine floats under the water's surface.

- Its ballast tanks are filled with water. Air is forced out of the tanks.
- The submarine has around the same density as the water. It does not sink, and it is not forced to the surface.
- The buoyant force is equal to gravity's force.

Glossary

ACCELERATION: to move faster and faster. Applying more force increases acceleration.

BUOYANCY: being able to stay afloat. A submarine does not sink because of its buoyancy.

COMPLEX MACHINE: a machine made from two or more simple machines. A bicycle is a complex machine.

ENERGY: the ability of something to do work. A moving car uses kinetic energy.

FORCE: a push or pull. Force changes the movement or shape of an object.

GRAVITY: a type of force that pulls objects toward Earth's core. Gravity keeps us on Earth's surface.

INERTIA: an object's resistance to changing its motion. Inertia keeps roller coaster cars moving up hills.

MAGNET: a piece of metal that attracts or repels other magnets and attracts some types of metal. Magnets attract and repel other magnets.

MAGNETIC FIELD: the area around a magnet that attracts or repels other magnets or attracts some metals. A strong magnet has a big magnetic field.

MOMENTUM: a moving object's momentum is its mass times its velocity, going in its direction of motion. A Nascar driver still has momentum even after the driver's car has crashed.

PROPULSION: the action of moving, pushing, or driving something forward, such as a train. Certain trains use the propulsion of magnets to move on a track.

ROTATION: motion that spins. Earth has rotation.

SIMPLE MACHINE: a basic tool that makes work easier by changing a force's direction or strength. The screw is a simple machine.

TRANSLATION: the movement of an object along a line or a curve. A soccer ball soars across the field in translation.

WORK: using force to get something done. Simple machines make it possible to do work with smaller forces.

Further Information

The Compound Machine
http://www.edheads.org/activities/odd_machine/index.shtml
This online animation shows how forces and simple machines combine to create a compound machine. Multiple choice questions throughout the activity test understanding.

DeRosa, Tom, and Carolyn Reeves. *Forces & Motion Student's Manual: From High-Speed Jets to Wind-Up Toys*. Green Forest, AR: Master Books, 2009.
Investigate forces and motion with the 20 projects in this book and track your results. This manual is designed as a journal for you to record your questions, ideas, and project results.

Marvin and Milo
http://www.physics.org/marvinandmilo.asp
At this Institute of Physics website, you can let the cat and dog team of Marvin and Milo guide you through some physics experiments.

Motion and Forces
http://www.learningscience.org/psc2bmotionforces.htm
This site has a variety of interactive lessons about physics.

Salas, Laura Purdie. *Discovering Nature's Laws: A Story about Isaac Newton*. Minneapolis: Millbrook Press, 2004.
Learn about Isaac Newton, the British scientist who changed physics and the world with his ideas, including his laws of motion.

Silverstein, Alvin, Virginia Silverstein, and Laura Silverstein Nunn. *Forces and Motion*. Minneapolis: Twenty-First Century Books, 2008.
Continue your exploration of the basics of physics with this book.

Suntrek: Satellites and Rockets
http://www.suntrek.org/solar-spacecraft/satellites-rockets/satellites-rockets.shtml
Explore satellites, gravity, rocket building, and orbiting Earth on this site created by several scientists in the United Kingdom.

Yasuda, Anita. *Explore Simple Machines! With 25 Great Projects*. White River Junction, VT: Nomad Press, 2011.
Do some hands-on learning with this book of projects using simple machines.

Index